# CONTENTS

# WHY A SPIDER?

If the thought of keeping spiders makes you feel queasy, you'd better stop reading now... But if you're still reading, get ready for a fascinating journey. You will be amazed by how much you can learn from these creatures.

All spiders are made of the same basic body parts. They have two large body segments, eight legs and two feelers.

Rear body segment, or **abdomen**.

Eight legs, each made of seven **segments**.

## WHAT IS A TARANTULA?

In this book, we look at tarantulas, which are the best spiders to keep as pets. They are large, hairy spiders that live very long lives – the females can live for 20 years or more. Like all spiders, they are **invertebrates**, which means that they do not have a backbone. They do not have any internal bones. Instead, their bodies are covered in an **exoskeleton** made of a material called chitin, which is strong but lightweight and waterproof.

**Pedipalps, or sex organs.**

Before you buy a tarantula, you must ask your family what they think about it. Keeping a spider is a big responsibility. They live for a long time, and you must care for the spider properly and keep it safe and secure. You will also need the help of an adult if the spider is injured.

**Front body segment, or cephalothorax.**

## DANGER ALERT: VENOMOUS BITE

All tarantulas have a **venomous** bite. Tarantula venom isn't deadly to humans, but a bite hurts as much as a bee sting. The best way to avoid being bitten by your tarantula is to be sure never to handle it.

Tarantulas have two sharp fangs that move up and down. They use their fangs to stab prey and pull it towards them.

# WHICH SPIDER?

Buy a **captive-bred** tarantula from a specialist breeder, not one that has been captured from the wild. Spiders that have been bred in captivity are less likely to be carrying **parasites**. Also, some **species** of tarantula are becoming rare in the wild, so it is best to leave wild spiders where they are.

Some tarantulas are more aggressive than others, so you must be careful when choosing your first one, and avoid aggressive species. It is best to choose a female. A male is likely to spend much of his time trying to escape from his home to find a mate. Females also live much longer than males.

Goliath birdeater has a **leg span** of up to 28 cm.

The stunning greenbottle blue tarantula digs burrows under bushes. It is fast-moving and aggressive, so is best left to experienced keepers.

The largest tarantula of all is the Goliath birdeater, which lives in the tropical forests of South America. Despite its name, it rarely catches birds.

## DANGER ALERT: IRRITATING HAIRS

In addition to a venomous bite, many tarantulas have a second means of defence. They throw their hairs at you! Called **urticating hairs**, the spiders throw these tiny spears by scraping their bodies with their rear legs. The hairs get stuck in the skin and can be very itchy.

This Mexican red knee tarantula has rubbed part of its abdomen bare of hairs.

## WHICH SPECIES?

All the tarantulas featured in our factfiles are relatively calm species that live on the ground in the wild. These are the best spiders for beginners, but the calmer species are also usually the ones that throw their hairs at you, so you must still take care.

# SPIDERS IN THE WILD

There are more than 40,000 species of spider, ranging in size from as small as a pinhead to as large as a dinner plate. All but one of these species are carnivores. They catch their prey either by ambushing them or by building webs to trap them.

Female black widow spiders have a distinctive red 'hourglass' marking on their abdomens. The male is half the size and brown in colour.

## BLACK WIDOW

The black widow spider has a highly venomous bite that it uses to kill insects. This spider takes its name from the females' habit of killing and eating the males after mating with them. This meal provides the female with extra energy, which she uses to help her make her eggs.

Orb-weavers finish their webs off with spirals of special sticky silk.

## SPINNING SILK

Spiders make silk from a special gland in their abdomens called a spinneret. Tarantulas use the silk to line their **retreats**, but many other spiders use it to make webs to catch prey. Orb-weaver spiders weave the complex wheel-shaped webs that you often find in gardens. They make a new web every day. In the evening, the spider eats the web, along with any flies caught in it.

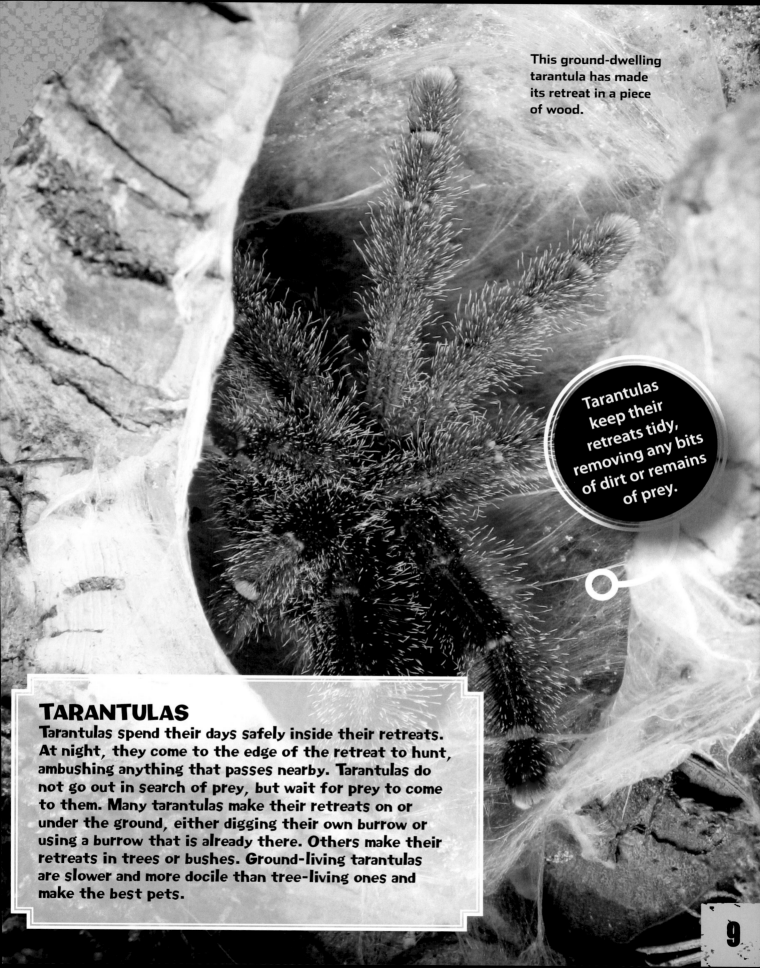

This ground-dwelling tarantula has made its retreat in a piece of wood.

Tarantulas keep their retreats tidy, removing any bits of dirt or remains of prey.

# TARANTULAS

Tarantulas spend their days safely inside their retreats. At night, they come to the edge of the retreat to hunt, ambushing anything that passes nearby. Tarantulas do not go out in search of prey, but wait for prey to come to them. Many tarantulas make their retreats on or under the ground, either digging their own burrow or using a burrow that is already there. Others make their retreats in trees or bushes. Ground-living tarantulas are slower and more docile than tree-living ones and make the best pets.

# A SAFE PLACE

A tarantula must be kept in a tank that is suitable for it to make a retreat. Tarantulas live on their own in the wild, and sometimes eat one another, so pet tarantulas should live in their own tanks.

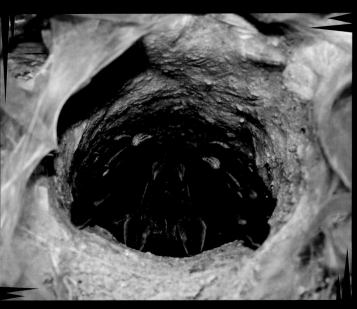

Tarantulas hunt by waiting at the entrance to their retreats and grabbing prey that wanders past.

## GLASS TANK

Tarantulas can be kept in a simple glass tank, or **terrarium**, about 2–3 times longer than the spider's leg span. It needs to be big enough for the spider to build a retreat. It is likely to treat a smaller tank as one large retreat and cover it in silk. For ground-living spiders, the tank should be no taller than 1.5 times the spider's leg span. Any higher than this and the spider may climb to the top and fall and injure itself.

This curlyhair tarantula has made its retreat under a piece of bark.

## TERRARIUM BASICS

Line the terrarium with a substrate of soil and mulch, about 5–10 cm deep, depending on the height of the tank. Always provide a bowl of water as this will stop the air from drying out. Make holes at the top of the terrarium to let the air in, but it should be securely closed to stop the spider from escaping. A temperature of 21–24°C is about right, but each species has its own requirements.

## SPACE FOR A RETREAT

For spiders that make their retreats in things they find, a pot broken lengthways is ideal. Half-bury the pot in the substrate. The spider will dig the soil out to make itself a retreat that is just the right size. Burrowing spiders need a deep substrate to dig into. Some burrowers need some help, and you may need to dig a burrow for them.

Some tarantulas make their retreats between the leaves of a tree.

# CHILEAN ROSE TARANTULA

## FACTFILE

Also called the Chilean common tarantula, this hardy spider is an ideal choice as a first tarantula. It is quite a docile, calm spider.

### TERRARIUM

The Chilean rose is a ground-dweller, so it does not need a tall terrarium. Give it a tank three times its leg span in length with a fairly dry substrate, a **hide** and a water bowl. The spider may try to dig a burrow, so make the substrate nice and deep. Keep the temperature above 20°C.

This spider has a bright pink **carapace**.

Males look very similar to the females, but males have hooks on the ends of their first pair of legs.

## IN THE WILD
This species is found in northern Chile, Bolivia and Argentina. It lives in burrows in desert and **scrub** areas, and hunts at night.

This spider is upset. It has reared up its front legs and may be about to flick its hairs.

## AGGRESSION
Look out for displays of aggressive behaviour. The spider is telling you to leave it alone.

This tarantula can have months when it does not eat and moves very little. This is normal.

**Lifespan of females:**
20 years

**Lifespan of males:**
3-7 years

**Leg span: 12 cm**

**Retreat: Digs its own burrow**

## FOOD
Feed your spider live crickets, mealworms or grasshoppers. Give it one or two insects per week, removing any that are uneaten after a day. (See page 14.)

**13**

# FEEDING YOUR SPIDER

Your spider will need to be fed live **prey**. A tarantula catches prey by responding to the prey's movement. Try to feed your spider a range of insects to ensure that they get all the nutrients they need.

## WHAT TO GIVE THEM

Not a lot is known about which nutrients spiders need from their diets, but a mix of the following will work: brown field crickets, mealworms and wax moth larvae (for spiderlings). Crickets should be the main staple of their diet.

In the wild, tarantulas eat many kinds of insect. This one has caught a cockroach.

Before offering them to your spider, leave crickets in a container with bran flakes in it overnight. This will make sure that the insects have been well fed, and will make a nutritious meal for the spider.

## HOW OFTEN?

Feed young tarantulas every 4–5 days, and adults about once a week. Choose prey that is just under half the spider's leg span in length. Give the spider one or two insects at a time, and remove any that are uneaten the next day. The spider will hunt and kill the prey one at a time, then gather them together into a ball, which it takes back to its retreat to eat. When a tarantula is due to shed its skin, it will stop eating for several weeks. Do not panic when this happens. Your spider will resume eating a few days after it has shed its skin.

## SENSITIVE LEGS

Tarantulas have very poor eyesight and cannot hear. They rely on special sense organs in their legs called slit sensillae. The slit sensillae pick up tiny vibrations in the ground made by the movement of nearby prey. These senses are so accurate that the spider can work out the exact size and location of the prey and pounce on it.

There should always be a water bowl in the terrarium. This is mainly to keep the humidity of the air high, but the spider will occasionally come out to have a drink.

# MEXICAN RED KNEE TARANTULA
## F A C T F I L E

The beautiful Mexican red knee tarantula is probably the most popular pet spider of all. It spends more time outside its retreat than other tarantulas, so you will be able to see it more often.

Both the females and males have striking orange markings on their legs.

## TERRARIUM

The red knee tarantula will adopt an artificial burrow that you provide as its retreat. It needs a substrate of peat or potting soil about 5 cm deep, which should not be allowed to dry out. Spiderlings need more attention than adults and should be checked regularly.

The tarantula will adopt a suitable space made by a piece of bark as its retreat.

**Lifespan of females: up to 25 years**

**Lifespan of males: 5–7 years**

**Leg span: 12 cm**

**Retreat: Makes a burrow in places it finds**

## FOOD

Feed live insects, as with other tarantulas. If you have a young spider, you will notice it becoming very fat between **moults**. This is normal, and if you want your spider to grow quickly, feed it regularly.

## IN THE WILD

This ground-dwelling spider is found in the mountains of Mexico, where it lives in forested areas. So many were caught from the wild for the pet trade that their numbers declined and exporting live spiders from Mexico has now been banned. However, breeding in captivity has been very successful, so you can buy captive-bred young spiders.

Young red knee tarantulas are a pale colour.

# CLOSE ENCOUNTERS

Most of the time, you will see your spider from the other side of the glass, but you will need to open the terrarium to feed it and remove dirt and remains. This is potentially a traumatic time for the spider, so ask and adult to help you.

## A SPIDER'S VIEW

Spiders experience the world in a very different way from us. They have very poor eyesight and rely primarily on their sense of touch. Remember that your spider may not see you coming, so be careful about approaching it suddenly. A tarantula is at its most dangerous when it is startled or frightened.

# HANDLING SPIDERS

Unlike other pets, spiders do not want to be handled by you and will not enjoy it. Tarantulas are also very fragile animals that are easily injured by falls – and your spider may fall if it tries to get away from you. It is best for both you and your spider if you enjoy your pet by looking at it, not touching it.

A tarantula's fangs are up to 3 cm long and very sharp.

## TARANTULA BITES

If the worst happens and your spider bites you, don't panic. Wash the area with warm water, then place ice on it for a few minutes. A bite hurts, but it is not usually dangerous unless you have an **allergic reaction**. A medicine called anti-histamine should stop it from itching.

This jumping spider has eight eyes, but like all spiders, its eyesight is poor.

## ESSENTIAL EQUIPMENT

A pair of large surgical tweezers, about 30 cm long, is an essential tool for a tarantula keeper. You can buy these from specialist reptile shops. Use them to feed your tarantula and clean its cage – they will keep your fingers well away from its fangs. Use a long-handled spoon to remove prey remains and add new substrate. Always use the tweezers or spoon to touch the spider, not your bare hands. Pay attention to what your spider is doing when you open the terrarium. It will probably back into its retreat, which is the safest place for it.

If your spider is a tropical species that likes humidity, spray the air with water from a pump spray bottle.

# THE MOULT

A spider's exoskeleton cannot grow or stretch, so in order to grow in size, a tarantula must moult. It grows a new exoskeleton under the old one, then sheds the old one. Spiderlings moult about once a month, while adults moult once every 1–2 years.

The old skeleton comes off in one piece.

## SIGNS OF THE MOULT

In the weeks leading up to a moult, your spider will become less active and may stop eating. Sometimes, depending on the species, a bald patch appears on the abdomen, which will darken. Make sure there are no insects in its terrarium at this time. A spider is totally helpless after shedding its old skin, and any insects may use the opportunity to take a bite!

A Chilean rose tarantula works its way out of its old skin. Be sure not to disturb your tarantula while it is moulting.

## DURING THE MOULT

Most tarantulas spin a silk sheet then lie on it on their backs to moult. They pop open their undersides and push the old skin up off their legs. Young spiders will recover within a day or two, but older ones may take weeks to get back to their old selves. Their new skin needs to dry and harden before they can eat as they replace their mouthparts during the moult.

Here, a fire-leg tarantula is lying on its back, pushing its skin up and off. It looks like two tarantulas lying on top of one another!

## MAKING REPAIRS

When it moults, a tarantula can repair damaged parts to its body. Any bald patches on its abdomen are covered in new hair, and it can even re-grow lost legs.

Take the old skin out of the terrarium when the spider has finished moulting. It will still be soft. Position it so that it looks like it is walking, and it will look like a real tarantula when it dries and hardens!

# COSTA RICAN ZEBRA
## FACTFILE

This tarantula takes its name from the cream-coloured stripes on its legs.

Also known as the stripeknee tarantula, the Costa Rican zebra is a hardy spider and a good choice for a beginner. It is a fast mover when it is annoyed, so you need to take care when opening the terrarium. It can flick urticating hairs, but prefers to run and hide.

## TERRARIUM

As a burrower, this tarantula needs a layer of substrate at least 10 cm deep. However, it may be reluctant to dig its own burrow in captivity, in which case you will need to dig one for it. Keep the terrarium warm, at **22–27°C** and keep humidity levels high with a supply of water.

**Lifespan of females:** up to 20 years

**Lifespan of males:** 4–5 years

**Leg span:** 10 cm

**Retreat:** Digs its own burrow

Males are darker in colour than females.

This spider's body is black or brown.

## IN THE WILD
This spider lives in open grassland areas in Central America. It does not live in deserts, and likes higher humidity levels than desert species. With lots of prey to catch, it grows quickly and reaches maturity within 2–3 years.

## FOOD
Feed the tarantula a variety of live insects, such as crickets.

# BREEDING SPIDERS

For experienced spider-keepers, the biggest challenge is to breed them. To do this, they meet up with fellow breeders who share their experience with them and, most importantly, share their spiders.

## MATCHING PAIRS

With so many species of tarantula, it is not always easy to tell the difference, especially as the males often look very different from the females. Introduce a male from another species to a female, and she will eat him for dinner! Breeders join tarantula societies, who help them to find the right mate for their spiders.

## COURTSHIP DANCE

The male is introduced to the female's tank to mate. This is a dangerous time for the male. If the female is not in the mood to mate, she may eat him. To put her in the mood, the male performs a dance, jiggling his body and tapping the ground. The spiders come together to mate, then straight away the male runs off. He knows she will not remain calm for long.

The smaller male (left) has special hooks on his front legs, which he hooks under the female's fangs to allow him to mate without being bitten.

The female will eat more than usual after mating to give her extra energy to produce the egg sac.

## SPIDERLINGS

Weeks or sometimes months after mating, the female lays an egg sac containing up to 1,000 eggs. About a month later, the eggs hatch into tiny spiderlings, which stay with their mother for a few weeks. The spiderlings then start to eat one another. This is normal! The strongest spiderlings survive, and are well fed on their brothers and sisters. The survivors are rehoused in their own homes.

These blue-footed tarantula spiderlings are ready to be rehoused.

# MEXICAN BLONDE TARANTULA

## FACTFILE

The Mexican blonde is a slow-growing tarantula that can reach an impressive size. It takes about 10 years to reach maturity, at which point the males die, but females can live for 20 years after this point. Females are a pale colour with dark legs, while the males are a bluish colour.

## IN THE WILD

The Mexican blonde lives in the deserts of southern Arizona and northern Mexico. It digs vertical burrows with round entrances, which it covers in a thin film of silk. For several months a year, it blocks up the entrance to the burrow and does not come out at all.

In summer, adult males travel large distances in search of females and are often seen crossing roads. This male has lost a leg during his travels.

**Lifespan of females: 30 years or more**

**Lifespan of males: up to 10 years**

**Leg span: up to 15 cm**

**Retreat: Digs burrows more than 60 cm deep in the soil**

The Mexican blonde has urticating hairs, but they are less irritating than the hairs of other tarantulas.

## FOOD

Feed the tarantula a variety of insects. Do not worry if your spider refuses to eat from time to time. They store fat in their abdomens and can easily go without food for months at a time, living off the fat.

## TERRARIUM

This is a very hardy spider with simple requirements. It needs nothing more than a deep sandy substrate and a water bowl to keep the humidity up.

# SPIDER FIRST AID

Very little is known about spider diseases, and you cannot take spiders to the vet. You may need to perform simple treatments and repairs at home. The most common problems come from falls or during the moult.

This whiteknee tarantula has black and white banded legs.

## PROBLEMS MOULTING

The moult is the most dangerous time in a spider's life. Sometimes it may get caught in its old skin, and you will need to cut it away using tweezers. If a spider loses a leg, do not worry too much. It will grow it back the next time it moults.

## KEEPING A RECORD

Keep a record of each time your spider moults, and keep the skins if possible. These will tell the story of your spider's life as it grows. They will also remind you of your spider when it has gone.

## REPAIRS

You'll need the help of an adult to look after your spider. If your spider is injured in a fall, holes in its exoskeleton can be mended with superglue. If a tarantula is bleeding, you can use non-medicated talcum powder to stem the flow. Tarantula blood is a pale blue colour.

This Brazilian whiteknee tarantula is in an attacking pose. Be very careful when treating spiders that you are not attacked.

## AMAZING SPIDER FACTS

Wolf spiders carry their young spiderlings on their backs.

Spider silk is five times stronger than a steel thread of the same diameter.

Some tarantulas spin a line of silk near the entrance to their burrows. This acts like a trip wire, alerting the spider to any potential prey that walks on it.

The tarantula hawk (below) is a wasp that captures tarantulas and feeds them to its young.

Female tarantulas continue to moult after reaching adulthood, but males do not. Once he has reached his full size, the male's job is to find a female and mate. He dies soon afterwards.

# SPIDER QUIZ

Test out your spider knowledge with this short quiz.

Can you indentify these four species of tarantula from their photos?

**I.**

**2.**

**3.**

**4.**

**5. What is the name for a spider's front body segment?**

**6. What is a spider's tough outer skin called?**

**7. What does a spider's spinneret do?**

**8. What are baby spiders called?**

**9. Give two reasons why you should you always buy captive-bred spiders?**

**IO. What has happened to the hairs on this tarantula's abdomen (below)?**

# GLOSSARY

**ABDOMEN**
The part of a spider's body that contains the lungs and the heart.

**ALLERGIC REACTION**
A response by the body to the presence of certain substances. It may cause swelling.

**BURROW**
A home that animals make for themselves by digging in the ground.

**CAPTIVE-BRED**
Born to parents that were kept by humans.

**CARAPACE**
The hard shell that protects the upper side of a spider's body. The carapace is part of the spider's exoskeleton.

**CARNIVORE**
An animal that eats other animals.

**CEPHALOTHORAX**
The part of a spider's body that contains the brain and jaws. The spider's legs and feelers are attached to the cephalothorax.

**EXOSKELETON**
A hard outer skin that protects and supports a spider's body.

**GLAND**
A part of the body that makes particular substances.

**HIDE**
A covered area a spider can move under so that it feels safe.

**INVERTEBRATE**
An animal that does not have a backbone. Insects and spiders are invertebrates.

**LEAF LITTER**
A layer of leaves that covers the ground in forests.

**LEG SPAN**
The length of a spider as measured from the ends of its legs.

**MOULT**
To shed an outer layer of the body.

**MULCH**
A layer of material such as bark that is placed on top of a layer of soil to keep the soil damp.

**PARASITE**
An animal or plant that lives on or inside another animal or plant, and often causes it damage.

**PEDIPALPS**
A pair of leg-like body parts at the front of a spider's head that it uses during mating.

**PREY**
An animal that is hunted by other animals for food.

**RETREAT**
The home a tarantula makes for itself.

**SCRUB**
An area in which small plants such as shrubs grow, but there are no trees.

**SEGMENT**
A distinct part to a spider's body. A spider has two main body segments, while each leg is made of seven segments.

**SILK**
A strong thread that spiders make in their bodies.

**SPECIES**
A kind of living thing. Members of the same species are able to reproduce with one another.

**SUBSTRATE**
Loose material used to line the bottom of a terrarium.

**TERRARIUM**
A special cage that a spider lives in, in which conditions are similar to those in the wild.

**URTICATING HAIRS**
Hairs on a tarantula's abdomen that it rubs off with its legs and throws at attackers.

**VENOMOUS**
Possessing a bite or sting that contains venom. The venom is injected into the body of the victim and makes it ill.

# USEFUL WEBSITES

**www.thebts.co.uk**
Website of the British Tarantula Society, with information about the care and breeding of tarantulas and an online forum where you can ask questions about tarantulas.

**www.tarantulas.com**
Photos and videos on all aspects of spider care and breeding. With links to further information, an online magazine, and specialist suppliers.

# INDEX